PICTURES · FROM · THE · PAST

Northern Life

PICTURES · FROM · THE · PAST

Northern Life

Frank Atkinson

COLLINS & BROWN

First published in Great Britain in 1991
by Collins & Brown Limited

Text Copyright © Frank Atkinson 1991

A CIP catalogue record for this book
is available from the British Library

ISBN 1 85585 067 2

The pictures in this book are archive photographs and, to preserve the character and
quality of the original, have not been re-touched in any way.

Acknowledgements
The author and publishers are grateful to the following for permission to reproduce
copyright photographs:
Frank Atkinson: 42 (bottom); Beamish North of England Open Air Museum, County
Durham: 1, 8 (far left), 15 (top), 25 (top), 42 (top), 43, 60, 69, 71, 80, 81; The Bede Gallery,
Jarrow: 67 (top).

All other photographs were supplied by the Hulton Picture Company and are available as
framed prints. For more information and to place your orders contact:

**Framed Prints
Hulton Picture Company
Unique House
21–31 Woodfield Road
London W9 2BA**

**Tel: 071 266 2660
Fax: 071 266 2414**

Conceived, edited and designed by Collins & Brown Limited,
Mercury House, 195 Knightsbridge, London SW7 1RE

Editor: Sarah Hoggett
Picture Research: Philippa Lewis
Art Director: Roger Bristow
Designed by: Gill Della Casa

Filmset by Tradespools Ltd, Frome
Reproduction by Butler & Tanner Ltd, Frome
Printed and bound in Great Britain by Butler & Tanner Ltd, Frome

CONTENTS

Introduction · 6

Domestic Life · 10

Country Life · 30

The North at Work · 50

The North at Play · 74

INTRODUCTION

Yet another book on the North? I'd like to think that this one is different. First and most importantly, let us be clear that there are many differences between the North and the South and this book is a celebration of those differences. Secondly, the period chosen – the 1920s to the 1950s – is one of great change and readers will find scenes and activities that are no longer with us, but are still part of every northerner's heritage. If this book seems nostalgic, why should it not be? Things do not have to be attractive or sweet-scented to be nostalgic. This writer can get nostalgic over a coky hydrogen-sulphide smell, reminding him as it does of his first experience of daily work at a coking and by-product plant at Crigglestone – and does not that name itself have a northern wrangle about it?

Every northerner has his own 'turning-on' image: perhaps the Liver Birds to a Liverpudlian, Tyne Bridge to a Novocastrian, Shap Fell to a Cumbrian, and every individual will have something personal linked to his past: often from childhood or from the time of a first love, a first job, visiting grandparents or holidays. And if these words appear to emphasize a sexist image, then perhaps that too was – maybe still is – northern. The Andy Capp image, however much it may be publicly deplored, is still occasionally with us in the North.

Most of the following photographs were taken forty, fifty or sixty years ago. Apart from the War which interrupted and altered so much, this period covers many dramatic changes, whether they be of social class, personal affluence, ready communications or loss of heavy industry. It was a time before the advent of television, which encouraged us all to try and live like everyone else and to want to buy the same things in the same shops. It was a

BELOW: *Scrubbing doorsteps in a Liverpool backstreet in 1954 – a back-breaking task.*

BELOW: *Mr Fred Mitchell, the proud owner of a Bradford cotton mill in 1912.*

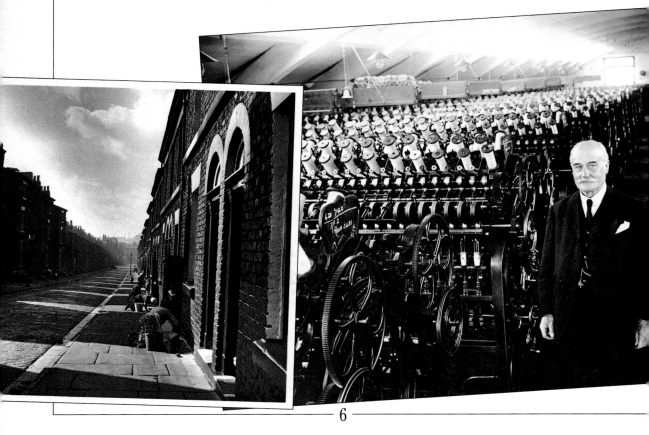

time, too, when physical labour and dirty jobs predominated in the area, when holidays meant a week at Blackpool or Scarborough or Whitley Bay; when your landlady decided whether you 'came in' or 'stayed out' during the day; times of sandcastles, rolled-up trousers, deck chairs, donkeys on the sand and strolls along the pier; the day of the Brownie box camera, when the only music on the beach would come from the pierrots or the occasional wind-up gramophone.

Then it was back home by train, until next year – to a cosy coal fire, flying ducks on the wall, a fret-fronted wireless in the corner, coconut matting on the floor; a Laurel and Hardy salt and pepper set on the table; salmon for tea, followed by pikelets.

Beyond the kitchen lay the backstreets: puddles, cobbles and mud, clothes-lines across the way and dribble-nosed toddlers. And the occasional street lamps around which the kids (you and I?) played at hopscotch or whip-and-

top or skipping, or if it were summer out into the nearby fields to chase butterflies, catch sticklebacks in the stream or play catty or kit-kat on the heath.

In the more rural parts (and to anyone from the South daring to read this, there were and still are enormous rural areas in the North) there might be the chance to help get in the harvest or go potato picking. Blackberrying was great fun, too. And you could see hay being carried, tied in rope bundles, piggyback to the hayloft if you lived in the Pennines; or you might help get it in on a horse-drawn dray or 'rolley'. And those moors, criss-crossed with black field-walls of gritstone, were the background to hound-trailing in the Lakes or knurr and spell in the Pennines. Sheep were, and still are, important on the fells, though they seem nowadays to be gathered in by men on motorcycles rather than on foot with dog and crook. Although we may look back at these countryside scenes with fond childhood memories, let us recall that it

BELOW: *Carthorses such as these, crossing Shap Fell in Cumbria, are rarely seen nowadays.*

BELOW: *Mr James Heywood, clog-maker, at work in Wigan in 1939.*

was hard grinding work for the farmer, who had to be out in all weathers, up before dawn and – in winter at least – working until dusk.

Back home the cinema had not yet been transmogrified into a Bingo Hall, providing fun for the kids on Saturday and warm privacy for lovers of an evening.

Saturday for the men might mean a match at Trafford Park or St James's Park, cleaning out the pigeons and packing them into baskets for their trip south, out with the whippets, pipe-smoking in the allotment, or down to the Club for a pint.

And Monday meant back to work, among the hundreds of tall black chimneys, down the cobbled lanes to the mill; across to the pit; or along the streets to the shipyard where the great hull rose above the house-tops and temporarily changed the view. Back to grime and toil and noise. Cotton mills had not yet been replaced by cheap imported cotton; coal was still needed to power the great steam engines, and

supply the multiplicity of households, all with smoking chimneys; and ships were still built on the Tyne and the Wear by the thousand tons at Palmer's, Swan Hunter and Pickersgills. In the fishing ports like Whitby the ships gathered, filling the scene with their masts; the dockside covered with fishing nets and lobster pots, or – if the fleet had just arrived – boxes of fish and the incomprehensible auctioneer.

For the women, few of whom went out to work once married with children, Monday meant washday: a hard time with posser and mangle, boiling water by the fire and followed by ironing with more hot work as the flatirons heated up on the fire. In some parts of the North scrubbing out the house and the steps was not sufficient, for the steps had also to be 'stoned' with scouring stone to give a smart cream-edged finish. Sometimes even the footpath (it wasn't a 'pavement' then) outside the front door would be scrubbed across.

Along the streets trundled tramcars, past the

BELOW: *The Durham Miners' Gala – sadly much reduced in size in recent years.*

BELOW: *Lakeland hound trailing: owners yell encouragement to spur on their dogs.*

pub at every corner, past the big Co-op shop, over the new-fangled crossing with its Belisha beacons, overtaking cyclists determined not to slip into the groove and horse-drays rattling along, passed by tooting cars and motorcycles. Horses were still to be seen everywhere in those not-so far-off days, drawing carts and pulling heavy loads.

At a street corner the newsboy yelled his wares; the Arcades stood welcoming with their arched glass roofs and pattern-tiled floors; and old ladies (or so they seemed), in their shawls and perhaps even clogs, went to and fro shopping or gossipping.

Away from the town centre, corner shops were the housewife's mainstay, ready to provide everything from clothes pegs and margarine to flour and 'yest' (or yeast) for breadbaking – and so back to the fire and the home again.

Of course much of this is a nostalgic view, warm and cosy at least in part, seen through the rosy glow of years long gone. And if we are honest with ourselves we shall also recall the hard physical labour, fear of long-term unemployment, death by machine or rock-fall, lack of hygiene, suffering of illness: diphtheria, tuberculosis, septicaemia and the terrible effects of back-street abortions.

The photographs which make up this book have been selected to show both the best and the worst of those times. The photographers themselves were trying to show what they found and no doubt on occasion they were trying hard to find the joyous, the sad, the grim, the amusing. So the task of making a modern selection has been far from easy, though fascinating in the extreme.

So much has changed for the better. Perhaps we should not brood too much upon what has gone before, but remember it for what it was, and be thankful that we don't have to go back to what are sometimes glibly referred to as the 'good old days'.

BELOW: *Happy theatre-goers outside a Newcastle theatre.*

BELOW: *'Tippit' – a traditional pub game. Great concentration is obviously required.*

DOMESTIC LIFE

Many a woman's work pattern would change over her life. After leaving school, but before marriage, she might go 'into service', or to the mill if she lived in the western side of northern England: there was less of such work if she lived in the east, where coal-mining did not so readily lend itself to woman's work.

Marriage changed her life completely, keeping house for her man, bringing up the children, and the coping with more working men in the household as her young ones went to work in turn.

A young woman who had been in service would often prove to be a good housekeeper, taking care in cleaning, skilled at cooking and building up a cupboardful of preserves and the like, watching the pennies.

Every penny counted and careful shopping was a necessity if an average wage of £2 per week was to cover rent, clothes and food. Holidays might not be so relatively expensive as they can be today, but still had to be saved for.

As the century wore on more and more young women were able to find work in offices and shops and even teaching. They were of course 'a cut' above the mill workers, would dress better, probably speak with less of an accent and seek a husband who did not need his back scrubbing at the end of his shift.

RIGHT: *In this Newcastle back street in 1959, washday apparently took precedence over the transport of toffee. And today's Trades Description Act would have something to say about the ingredient the manufacturers claimed to be in that toffee.*

LEFT: *In the steep cobbled back street, skipping with abandon, two young sisters sing happily, the sun reflecting on the wet shiny stones running unevenly underfoot down to other streets and backyards below.*

Their elder sister, after being on short time at the mill, has been 'stood off' for a fortnight. She tries to enter into their spirited play but can only think about tomorrow ... and tomorrow. Will the mill start again and if not ... what ...?

ABOVE: *In the poorer streets of Ordsall in 1950, a group of children gather round a street musician. At that time there were few opportunities for such children to stretch themselves in play: no play areas, no green fields. From time to time efforts were made by benevolent groups to take children from these poor surroundings and give them a glimpse of the countryside: its sights, sounds and smells. But although such holiday schemes helped to alleviate the worst of slum and town life for a time, they did nothing to change it.*

FAR LEFT: *In some respects, this country scene has changed little since it was photographed in the early 1950s. Haworth, home of the Brontë sisters, still has a steep cobbled street with irregular buildings holding tight together. Doubtless the increased wealth brought by tourists has penetrated every cottage to some extent, even if the pressure of numbers has also changed a quiet way of life.*

LEFT: *Depressed to the point of inactivity, this poor woman in a rotting house in South Shields sits before her tiny fire, surrounded by damp walls, with inadequate food and without the will to do anything about it. These conditions were not uncommon in the 1930s, when this picture was recorded as part of a move towards slum clearance.*

BELOW: *By contrast the farm labourer and his wife, photographed in 1940, seem to live in better conditions than those of an urban slum dweller: with a clean and tidy fireplace, easy chairs, reasonable clothing and able to enjoy a relaxed evening together.*

LEFT: *Mrs Elizabeth Margaret Braddock JP was a noted member of Parliament – and a local Councillor – for part of Liverpool. She was known nationally as Battling Bessie Braddock and recognised as a turbulent character even in a city where passions could run high. This glimpse of a queue of constituents waiting to see her in 1954 gives an impression of the serious problems which they brought to her.*

ABOVE: *This picture was published in November 1940, in an article highlighting the problem of a family of seven in a midlands town, now accommodating a further four children brought here as evacuees.*

Such wartime overcrowding was not the only problem, for some evacuees from very poor homes brought with them, particularly into the countryside, a variety of diseases including impetigo and 'nits' (head lice), as well as being a disruptive element in a community which was often quite alien to them: no street lights and no fish and chips.

LEFT: *Family teatime in a Lancashire cotton town which was enjoying a sudden boom in 1955. Only the man on the right does not work in the local mill: all the rest are associated with it in some way.*

BELOW: *Somewhere along Tyneside a photographer recorded this everyday moment in 1950. Today those single-storey cottages will long have gone; young women will be seen in slacks or jeans, and certainly without head scarves. Prams have been replaced by buggies and housewives would hardly walk with their children down the middle of the street today. Similarly the dog would have to be on a lead for the street will be carrying heavy traffic.*

RIGHT: *What a curious picture, taken perhaps in the 1940s. Two well-dressed children, led by their smart father, walk down the muddy back lane between rows of tumble-down workers' houses, watched in some amazement by the local kids. The contrast is stark and one cannot help thinking that the photographer 'laid it all on' for this dramatic effect. Yet whether or not he was justified in doing this, the photographer's record highlights the gulf between the well-to-do and the workers.*

A Woman's Work . . .

When scrubbing extended to the pavement is it any wonder that people said 'A woman's work is never done'? Every day of the week had its duties: clothes washing, baking, ironing, dusting and polishing.

FAR RIGHT: *To a modern young (part-time) housewife this photograph must be almost unbelievable. Taken in 1944, it also shows an air raid shelter at the end of the street.*

RIGHT: *Around 1950 the Mayor of Nelson, Lancashire, set up a voluntary service to provide companionship for old and lonely people. Here is one of the visitors making tea for her elderly host in the tiny kitchen.*

BELOW: *'Now which one was I wanting?' In 1955 named margarine was back on the market. Only two years earlier it was still 'national', as it had been throughout the war.*

LEFT: *Taking the children to school has long been one of a mother's duties, though now many go in their own cars. This wet street was in Scotswood, a poor suburb of Newcastle-upon-Tyne, in October 1950.*

RIGHT: *School milk was provided for children at a halfpenny per third of a pint in 1934. In one month, it is recorded, the amount supplied to British schools was almost two million gallons. It became free in 1939, but now…? (Do you remember cardboard milk bottle tops?)*

BELOW: *In 1956, when this photograph was taken, teachers were in revolt; controversy over pension contributions had been the last straw. Overcrowded classrooms and extra duties all sapped their energies and enthusiasm. Yet here, in a primary school in Hulme, a teacher finds time for a little personal attention.*

ABOVE: *In 1952 the Lancashire cotton workers were in dire straits with 60,000 operatives on part-time or out of work. The cotton towns had permanent cheap cut-price sales of goods they had made. But there was no money to buy even at these prices. This shop window was in Rochdale.*

LEFT: *As always, though perhaps more so than today, where you shopped depended on who you were. This is the James Street shopping centre of Harrogate in 1938, where parking had not yet become a major problem. The hydro town was flourishing and ladies in splendid hats had plenty of time on their hands.*

FAR LEFT: *'Bringing up a very big family' is the 1945 caption of this startling picture; 'Fifteen-year-old Mary is the eighth in this big and happy Yorkshire family' runs the simple message. She is busy cleaning one of her brother's clogs, with its heavy iron sole and heel plates.*

LEFT: *United Cattle Products provided a wide range of foodstuffs for the poorer household: meat and potato pies at 3d each (roughly a modern penny) and sausage rolls at 1d each (or 5 modern pence per dozen). How about a cowheel pie . . . today?*

BELOW: *No more does the retired pipe-smoker need to buy a pair of working clogs, each one brightened by the brass nails holding the leather upper to the wooden sole.*
Wigan in the 1940s was possibly not too bad if your desires were not set too high and at least the old man, sans teeth, has a clean muffler and appears to have a golden sovereign on his watch chain.

COUNTRY LIFE

Working life in the country could be no less arduous than in industry: up before dawn, out in all weathers with none of today's 'protective clothing'.

Whilst work changed with the seasons it also differed according to the terrain: sheep on the fells, grain and cattle on the lower land. A man would generally stay in the same kind of work all his life, sometimes going to the annual hiring fair to change his employer. While we may think of this country work simply as manual and unskilled, this was far from the truth. Many of these skills have now virtually disappeared, such as the care of heavy horses, their medicinal treatment and their breeding; laying a hedge, and even forking up on to the haycart and thatching the stacks, required skills now gone. Shepherding has probably changed much less, though mopeds seem to be taking the place of boots and crook.

If by 'country life' we are thinking of such leisure activities as chasing indigenous wildlife, then apart from the loss of some more noticeable cruelties such as the hunting of otters and badgers, that way of life has probably changed little. Hunts still meet and grouse are still shot. Less bloodthirsty, but undoubtedly exhausting, is hound trailing, which can still be seen and enjoyed in the Lake District.

RIGHT: *Tynedale is one of the more dramatic scenic areas of the Pennines, rising near the Cheviots on the Scottish border and flowing more than eighty miles mostly through beautiful countryside, before coming to industrial Tyneside.*

Here near Kielder – now the site of Britain's largest man-made lake – this youngster is carrying a fleece from a long-haired sheep.

LEFT: *A Morris Cowley 'Bullnose', perhaps with dickey seat behind. A number of details help to date this example quite closely: no front wheelbrakes are discernable so it is pre-1926; the beaded edge tyres suggest pre-1924, and the three-lamp lighting suggests early 1920s. On the driver's running board is a petrol can, probably by Pratts, with a brass cap.*

The car is unusually well-supplied, having two spare wheels, advisable in view of the road surface on those hilly little-used roads: possibly in the Buttertubs area between Swaledale and Wensleydale.

ABOVE: *Another twenties photograph, of January 1923. The High Peak Harriers, meeting at Buxton. Lady Rachel and Lady Anne Cavendish are in the centre, so an old caption tells us; the latter is carrying a long dog whip. Harrier hounds, not seen here, have much in comon with the foxhound and the beagle.*

Hunting the hare is not so common a sport as once it was, hares themselves being rather rarer than they were earlier in the century. The Encyclopaedia of Sport *(1911) informs its readers that the 'amount of sport which the hare provides in the shape of hunting, coursing and shooting demands some effort for its proper protection'.*

LEFT: *1947 was a year of heavy snow, proving to be a great ally of foxes in Yorkshire – so much so that the increasing number of foxes became a great threat to newborn lambs.*

Many farmers moved against their old enemy and here we see a party of farmers setting off with their guns on Grassington Moors. The man in the centre looks as though he may pose a threat to his fellow hunters.

ABOVE: *'It is not mere blood lust which encourages men and women to hunt the otter, but a true love and joy in the myriad sights and sounds of the countryside.' So it was written in 1955 when this picture was taken of the huntsman of the Kendal and District Otter Hounds, holding up a freshly killed otter.*

RIGHT: *The daring 'egg-climmers' of Bempton cliffs on the East Yorkshire coast (though no doubt they saw it as an everyday job), are here in 1945 having a bite of lunch before descending again to collect the eggs of the guillemot which nests on ledges high above the sea. Collecting ceased in 1953.*

Hound Trailing

Hound trailing can draw great crowds in the Lake District, as seen in these photographs from 1951. An aniseed drag takes the puppies over a 5-mile run and the older dogs over a gruelling 10-mile mountain-side course.

ABOVE: *Like most sports the bookmakers have joined in the fun, taking bets from the crowd, even during the race. Hundreds of men came together in the fifties, though today it has become more of a family affair.*

LEFT: *Farm workers and countryfolk often bring one of their own hounds to take part. Perhaps for those not too anxious to expend energy, the pleasure lies in watching the hounds racing madly across the fells.*

RIGHT: *Owners, followers and their hounds were arriving at Troutbeck in September 1951, as they had done for years. It was – and still is – a big event in the Lakes and hounds are trained through the year.*

LEFT: *The difficulties facing Lancashire hill farmers in the fifties were immense. In part they were being met by special subsidies but one by one the higher farms were becoming deserted. It was (and still is) a rough hard job, out in all weathers and at all hours, perhaps alone apart from your trusty dog. These self-reliant men and their wives are still to be found on the little hill farms, but for how much longer can they survive?*

ABOVE: *Possibly one of the last photographs taken (in 1945) of the 'oldest Labour Exchange in the country': Carlisle Hiring Fair. This had taken place for many years at Whitsun and November, when farmers wanting labour could go to a little island site in the main street of Carlisle where labourers from all over the country gathered to sell their labour for the next six months.*

Here the farmer (right) talks with a prospective hire, who has come down from the Cumberland fells with his cape strapped across his shoulder. After about 10 minutes a deal has been made. The farmer will now pay the labourer 2s.6d ($12^1/_2$p) to seal the bargain.

ABOVE: *Getting in the hay is possibly more nostalgic to would-be country dwellers than any other rural occupation, and those who are old enough to have taken part as children will remember the warm-but-not-too-hot June and July, and the delicious scent of new-mown hay.*

RIGHT: *On the hills above the Calder Valley near Halifax, Frank o'Sands (always known by the name of his farm) and his sister rake the hay into 'ricklins' – part of the process of drying, gathering and carrying the hay into the barn as winter feed for the cattle.*

FAR RIGHT: *Today our milk is delivered in bottles, generally after pasteurisation. In the 1930s it was ladled into your jug in a tin pint-scoop straight from the churn. And how thrilled was a little boy who could help.*

BELOW: *A thoughtful word of advice from a driver to his helper. Buying, selling and showing off horses is at the heart of Brough Hill Fair and anyone who thinks he knows horses wants to be there. But* caveat emptor *when dealing with the horse-traders.*

RIGHT: *Brough Hill Fair in Westmorland is the place where gypsies and horse-dealers gather annually from all over the country. In 1950 there were still many colourful horse-drawn caravans and a noisy spectacle of trotting horses, shouting men and gossiping gypsy women. Doubtless the locals hate it and many worry about thefts from their backyards but it is now an attraction for holiday-makers.*

Sheep Farming

Northern sheep farming is an upland activity. The sheep, bred for these conditions, are also 'hefted' to the farmland: a kind of flock-knowledge by which they do not stray unduly on the high open fellsides and can find good shelter in bad weather.

FAR RIGHT: *Sheep are 'dipped' to destroy a parasite which burrows into the skin, weakening the animal and damaging its fleece. Romantic it may look, working on a hill farm in summer, but not on a bleak cold day at the sheep fold.*

RIGHT: *Sheep in a Cumberland farmyard gathered for shearing. The fleeces are then packed off for cleaning and spinning.*

BELOW: *There are many breeds of sheep in Britain. These are Herdwicks, the hardiest of all breeds, thriving upon poor mountain land and recorded here at Kentmere, Westmorland (now Cumbria).*

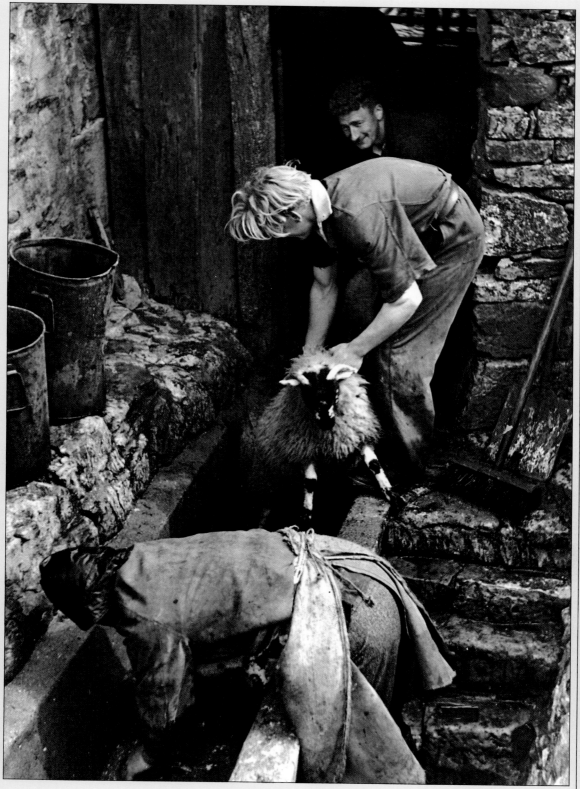

ABOVE: *Had the tup got out among the flock too early last year? These New Year arrivals at a farm near Whitehaven in Cumberland in 1936/7 were unusual, for lambs are not usually born in the north until late in January or even later on the hills. Achieving a suitable time of birth for lambs is always tricky: too early and the weather may kill them off; too late and the fattened lambs may miss the best of the market prices.*

RIGHT: *At the end of shearing, in late September, the clipped wool is bundled up into sacks ready for despatch. Here, at a farm at Catlow in Lancashire, the sacks were being stitched up. Sacks of this size have been used for several centuries and an eighteenth-century phrase for the price of wool was 'a penny a pound is a pound a pack': a play on the two meanings of 'pound' – weight and price – for the sacks weighed 240 pounds (109 kg) and there were 240 pence in a pound sterling.*

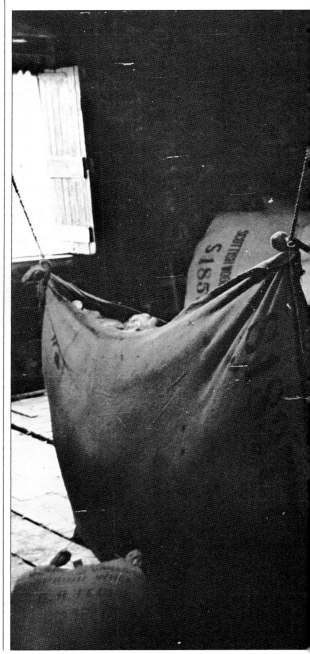

THE NORTH AT WORK

Heavy engineering, steel-making, ship-building and coal-mining are disappearing from the national scene, at any rate in the form and on the scale we would have found them in the middle of the century, less than fifty years ago. Steam power was then still an important prime mover: mills were driven by it, coal-mine shafts were wound by it, trains were hauled by it. All this used coal in large quantities and the iron industry required even more, in the form of coke, for the smelting process. Moreover, we all had coal fires in our homes and used these for heating, cooking, baking and washing.

These dangerous, grimy, physically arduous, yet skilled jobs occupied a large workforce spread across the North, each with its closed communities with their own traditions, folk memories and superstitions: a man would not go down the pit if he met a woman as he went to work, for example, nor would he whistle whilst underground. Team work by a group of 'marrers' or mates was essential and a workman's very life often depended on such mutual trust.

RIGHT: *Hull, a busy fishing port with more than 160 trawlers working from it, was responsible in 1951 for nearly half the fish eaten in Britain. Though the War had been over for six years, meat was still severely rationed, so fish became ever more important.*

Here filleters are at work on the Hull quayside, preparing a recent catch for sale, while trawlers are moored nearby.

FAR RIGHT: *Some of the ways up from the Tyne quayside towards the centre of Newcastle can look grim whether one is a worker, as here, or a modern tourist. Cobbles remain even today on some of these steep little-used streets and the massive masonry looks as though it will last forever.*

RIGHT: *In the early 1940s this would have been a farewell kiss as the soldier went to war. In 1947 it is more likely to be that of a worker off to a possibly disagreeable or dangerous job and the clothes support the idea – though whether many northern workers, even in 1947, parted this way may be open to doubt. Photographers can be very persuasive!*

BELOW: *People regularly going to work on trains, ferries, or even gondolas in Venice, have their set routines. Here the morning paper played its part on the Liverpool Ferry between Wallasey and Birkenhead in 1954. Today the ferry is still running, but for tourists now, with commentary.*

RIGHT: *From Glue Terrace, named after a once-flourishing (and no doubt smelly) works nearby, we can see Elswick Colliery. Although this photograph was taken in 1950, the colliery had closed in 1942. Nowadays when works close they are quickly demolished, scrapped and cleared (making it much more difficult for future industrial archaeologists!).*

This area has been considerably improved in recent years, with a broadened Scotswood road carrying much east-west traffic.

ABOVE: *A sight of the bridges of Newcastle-upon-Tyne brings a lump into the throat of many a long-asbent Geordie. Nearest is the Tyne Bridge, opened in 1928 and a strong symbol for the town, as it brings traffic into the centre of Newcastle along the A1. Next in height is the High Level Bridge, built by Robert Stephenson in 1844 and still carrying rail traffic on top and road traffic below. Between the two, crosses the Swing Bridge (1876), originally operated by hydraulic engine. Seen in the distance is the old Redheugh Bridge which was replaced in 1983.*

ABOVE: *An amusing glance at Manchester Royal Exchange in 1938. Already this property was 'To Let', as business requirements changed. And what sort of confidence is being exchanged here between these two well-dressed businessmen? The bushy moustache, pipe, hard bowlers and waistcoats could not be of any other time.*

LEFT: *This photograph, the original 1950 caption tells us, shows miners who have just completed a shift down Heworth Colliery. It is surprising to see these miners not rushing home to bathe, but perhaps they were waiting for a bus. Not all collieries provided pit-head baths at that time.*

The River Tyne

From Newcastle downstream to the Shields, the banks of the Tyne have traditionally been covered by quayside, shipyards, docks, engineering works and other industrial buildings. Modern changes have been dramatic.

LEFT: *West of the city centre this terrace ran down to the Tyne, with the power station (now closed) beyond.*

RIGHT: *On the quayside at North Shields near the mouth of the Tyne. From here many vessels put out into the North Sea fishing grounds.*

BELOW: *Boat building in the 1950s was still fairly flourishing in places, though by modern standards it was probably overmanned and troubled by demarcation disputes.*

BELOW: *Women played a role in northern labour activities long before 'Womens Lib' became a popular movement. Here in 1953 is a group about to take part in 'Durham Women's Labour Gala'.*

RIGHT: *Littlewoods football 'pools', which employed a staff of thousands at Liverpool in the mid-1950s, paid out a weekly dividend of over £400,000. Here several of the 'girl clerks' are relaxing during a break.*

LEFT: *A happy worker with an armful of cotton spindles snapped in Wigan in 1939 recalls more prosperous times for that industry. Whether one is better off with unemployment or with a noisy somewhat unsafe manufacturing environment is debatable.*

RIGHT: *At the Wednesbury works of J.H. Barlow, a local steel magnate, Mr Barlow is seen inspecting his works in 1950. Such prosperous and practical businessmen seem to be seen around less frequently today.*

BELOW: *More cotton spindles. Here they are being wound by machinery which would probably not be acceptable to today's Factories Inspectorate, whose standards have gradually increased over the years.*

LEFT: *At Ellington Colliery (Northumberland) in 1951, and now long closed, these men are about to ride to the surface at the end of their eight-hour shift. Grimy and grim-faced, exhausted and waiting for a sight of the sky, they crouch pitman-fashion on their 'hunkers'. Even at that time, three years after nationalization, two of them have been working without safety helmets, probably at the pit bottom.*

ABOVE: *Ponies are very rarely worked underground in British collieries today. This 1934 picture shows a stableman with one of his ponies which has just returned from an eight-hour shift in a Durham coal mine.*

Ponies were stabled underground to save the time and expense of raising them each day. They would be brought up annually at the time of the pit holiday, when they would roll around in the grass, excited at being free for a time. Yet they were well groomed, stabled and fed by generally caring men.

The Jarrow March

It was 5 October 1936 and 200 unemployed men set off from Jarrow on the banks of the Tyne, on a quixotic journey to present a petition to Parliament. They had all been unemployed for some time: the 1930s were dismal years and no town suffered more than Jarrow, where at one time 74 per cent of all the workers there were unemployed.

RIGHT: *'The town that was murdered': the words of Jarrow's MP Ellen Wilkinson, here leading off the Jarrow March with Councillor Dave Riley (in bowler) whose determination and administrative skill held the whole thing together.*

LEFT: *The Mouth Organ Band (trained by Tosh Core, far right), led the March. The mouth organs were given by Press reporters.*

BELOW: *The logistics and organisation of the March worked admirably, and a hot evening meal invariably met the marchers on their arrival. Here the men had hot corned beef and potatoes on a farm at Lavender near Bedford.*

ABOVE: *Pitmen coming off shift in the early 1940s. The conditions, even above ground, were dirty and harsh, with noise and escaping steam. The men are wearing cloth caps: nowadays they wear 'hard hats' which also hold the electric lamps, and their working conditions are safer, though still far from congenial.*

RIGHT: *Durham Miners' Gala (locally pronounced 'gayla') is still held each year, though as the number of mines has been drastically reduced, so has the number of 'lodges'. This picture, probably taken in the 1930s, shows Old Elvet as the crowds move towards the Race Course where the speeches would be held.*

LEFT: *Lime Street Station, Liverpool, in 1954. It does not seem long ago that these hand-drawn luggage trolleys were replaced by electrically-drawn trailers, though they had been in use since the middle of last century.*

BELOW: *Well-staffed rural railway stations in the 1930s provided plenty of labour for gardening between trains, and great was the pride in these well-tended bright flower beds. Tow Law station in lower Weardale became a keen competitor when 'best-kept' competitions were established.*

BELOW: *Whitby quayside, seen here around 1950 with some of the fishing fleet in, looks superficially the same today. But now there are fewer boats, more mechanization and many more tourists, here for the 'atmosphere' of a fishing port.*

RIGHT: *Two of the men who, in 1955, sailed on one of the fishing vessels working out from Fleetwood on the west coast of Lancashire. The skipper (right) and a member of his crew take a break before spending the next week tossed around in a vessel measuring 120 ft (36.6 m) long by 21 ft (6.4 m) on the beam.*

THE NORTH AT PLAY

Since rail travel could be relatively expensive and travel abroad was practically unheard of, holidays were generally taken fairly near at hand and families would return every year to Blackpool or Scarborough while some seaside communities would move inland to a small market town and its surrounding countryside.

Holidays at the seaside generally took the same form: on the beach playing in rockpools or building sand-castles, riding on donkeys or just sitting idly in deck chairs.

Whilst some aspects of northern leisure might have had much in common with other parts of the country, northern traits can certainly be identified in some weekend and evening relaxations such as growing leeks, keeping and racing pigeons or whippets, or going down to the pub or the club of an evening.

Many sports were somewhat more participatory than now, though sports grounds and teams were supported and followed. Some participatory sports were beginning to wane, such as cycle riding and racing.

The cinema and the music hall were popular and the Saturday matinée must have helped to keep many an overwrought mother sane. Before TV the music hall provided active entertainment, though many families would remain at home, glued to their wireless and listening to such favourites as ITMA and Arthur Askey.

RIGHT: *Relaxation, for many northcountry working men, has meant – and still does mean – drinking beer in a Working Men's Club. The first such Club was inaugurated in 1862 and in 1955, when this photograph was taken, there were over 3,000 clubs with a total of well over two million members.*

Then, as probably now, Durham led with the highest membership of any county. This particular photograph was taken at Langley Moor, just outside Durham City.

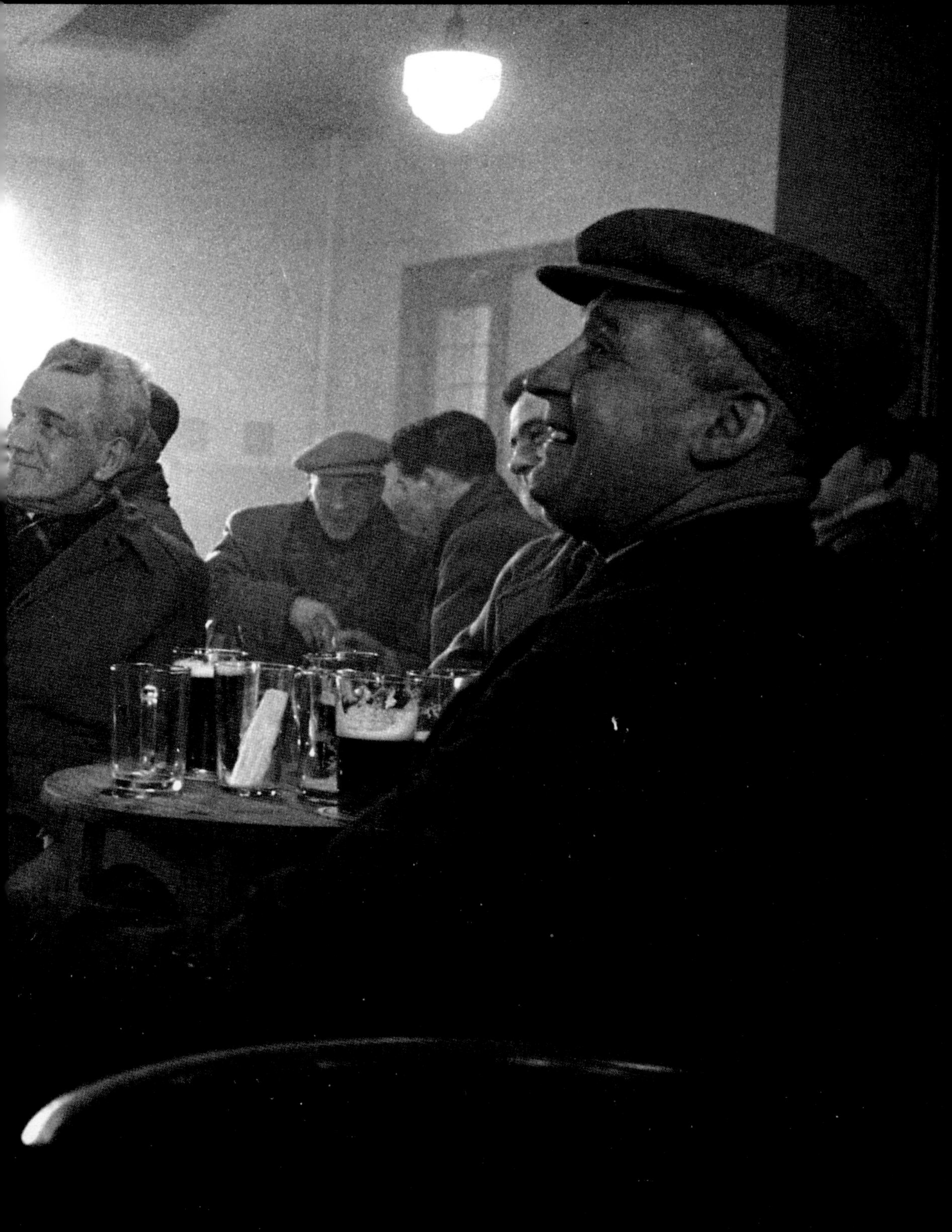

TOP AND ABOVE: *Working Men's Clubs now allow women too, though this must have restricted some of the expressions which 'men only' accepted among themselves.*

At a slightly earlier time these clubs offered an escape for the working man not only from his workplace but also from his wife and family. In social terms it probably offered a mid-way transition for men engaged in heavy manual work: mining, engineering and ship-building. The conditions of the all-male rough tough environment of work had to be slightly softened before he could easily take part in home life with his wife and children.

BELOW: *In a corner of Langley Moor Working Men's Club, a dog is being tempted by the Club's own brand of beer.*

The 'Fed' as it is familiarly called, or Federation Brewery, came into being in 1919. It provides for most clubs and is able to offer a good price to them, thereby helping to keep up their buildings and services, while providing a reasonably priced pint to their members.

RIGHT: *Before the advent of television the cinema provided escape from so much of life.*

Here, outside the Odeon Cinema in Manchester, the photograph says it all: dark wet streets, bright lights, tramcars arriving, people gathering before moving into the warm close upholstered atmosphere of the cinema.

The ex-Mrs Bradford was a crime comedy of 1936 starring William Powell and Jean Arthur.

ABOVE: *This splendid paste-up of old theatre posters and portraits recalls the time, at the Shakespeare Theatre in Liverpool, when well-known characters would 'play the Halls' week after week. Top right is a reference to 'Comedians on Parade, 1948', starring Frank E. Franks, a well-known County Durham comedian. And the poster held by the theatrical admirer refers to Bob and Alf Pearson who took part in Ted Ray's Ray's a Laugh (started by the BBC just after the war). Bob played the little girl, Jennifer.*

ABOVE: *Leek shows were – and still are – serious affairs, for a lot can depend upon the outcome. Here the judge carefully measures the circumference of a potential winner. The size of the leek is not the only criterion, but it is very important.*

LEFT: *As this 1952 photograph illustrates, vegetable shows praise the sheer size of produce. This has led, on occasion, to malicious damage to growing vegetables in competitors' gardens. The secrets of feeding and encouraging vegetable growth are much prized too.*

LEFT: *Here is a puzzle. Why is this brass band practicing on open moorland? The photographer's original caption hardly helps: 'Pennine Walking Tour, c.1947'.*

Brass bands have played a significant part in cheering up life in the North and nothing is more nostalgic than that characteristic sound drifting across the town park. They have led miners' gala parades, played on many formal occasions and (happily now including young people and all smartly dressed), are undergoing a rejuvenation.

RIGHT: *'Playground of the North' was Blackpool's sobriquet in 1949 when this picture was taken from the Tower.*

At that time, when travel abroad was almost unheard of by most families, the attraction of Blackpool was considerable. It provided everything one could desire: good sand, a promenade, a pier, a fairground and a Tower with ballroom, with Reg Dixon at the organ. Even the Blackpool landladies were involved in a love/hate relationship as families came back year after year.

ABOVE: *A closer view of those masses on the Blackpool beach, where some are seated in rented deckchairs enjoying a summertime snooze while others buy ice cream from the latest streamlined ice-cream van. People can probably be classified in terms of their view of crowds: those who like to be close together and those who only feel happy when no-one else is in sight.*

BELOW: *Way back in 1934, pleasure boats at Blackpool were being hauled over the beach for about half a mile down to the sea, following down the morning low tide. The leisure industry, as we would term it today, has grown since then, though heavy horses are sadly no longer in service.*

ABOVE: *Wakes Week was a northern institution, now less regularly adhered to as the activities of the various towns diversify from their single industries. This family-and-friends group was making the most of its Lancashire Wakes Week, at Blackpool in 1955. Perhaps it is partly a matter of weather, but it took a long time before northern menfolk shed their trousers before going into the sea.*

LEFT: *What can one say, except that people on holiday do sometimes relax to an unexpected degree. Blackpool (in 1955), extended an invitation to old-age pensioners (senior citizens, we would euphemistically call them today) in certain boroughs all over England, to enjoy a free week's holiday at the beginning of the season: hence the excitement.*

RIGHT: *Butlin's Camps made a name for themselves after the War, offering a well-organized activity holiday at a reasonable price. Today price matters slightly less and the degree of organization, as applied to the 'campers', is not so acceptable. However in 1953 people were obviously prepared to act the fool as a form of relaxation.*

BELOW: *All was not serious even in mid-War. Blackpool in August 1942 still offered donkey rides, as well as a Fun Fair and the usual games on the sand.*

Pigeon Racing

The working man's sport of pigeon racing is still quite popular in the North, though probably not so much as it was in the 1950s when more than two million pigeons raced annually in Britain and more than £500,000 was won in prize money.

FAR LEFT: *Careful breeding and pigeon care would take up all a fancier's spare time.*

LEFT: *In their baskets pigeons were carefully transported by rail to a far destination where they were released to fly back to their home lofts. Today similar journeys are made by specially converted big road vehicles.*

BELOW: *As far back as 1924 'The Pigeon Special' ran weekly from Newcastle-upon-Tyne to Kettering, carrying up to thirty thousand birds. They were carried in special pigeon baskets, seen here being loaded into the goods van.*

RIGHT: *Boxing, now seen as potentially damaging, is more carefully controlled than ever before. In the 1950s it was still a skill worth acquiring and boys were encouraged to take it up as a manly sport. It was on this basis that the Liverpool Police were organizing coaching sessions in youth clubs to keep the boys 'off the streets' and out of mischief, as seen in this 1954 photograph.*

RIGHT: *Wembley Stadium in 1928, as Healless, Captain of Blackburn Rovers, holds aloft the F.A. Cup after their victory over Huddersfield Town. Judging by the closed capes of the police it was rather a wet afternoon.*

BELOW: *The weather was fine and sunny at Manchester in July 1936, and early arrivals whiled away the time before the match began. This was the occasion of the Second Test Match between England and All-India.*

ABOVE: *A powerful photograph, dating from as recently as 1959, of a child at the window of a Liverpool slum – dark, damp and no doubt overrun by rats.*